You Married
THE
WRONG PERSON!

THE RELATIONSHIP SECRET
EVERY COUPLE NEEDS TO KNOW

TIM LUCAS

YOU MARRIED THE WRONG PERSON
© 2015 by Tim Lucas

Published by Liquid Church.
ISBN: 978-0-9863058-0-1
eISBN: 978-0-9863058-1-8

Cover Design by Daliborka Mijailovic
Typeset by Steven Plummer

Printed in the United States of America.

Dedicated to my wife Colleen.

I see Jesus more clearly because of you.

Contents

Preface

My wife and I were happy for 20 years. Then we met.
- RODNEY DANGERFIELD

As a pastor, I've officiated dozens of weddings. On the Big Day, I've noticed the bride can typically only focus on three things:

The Aisle, where the bride makes her grand entrance.

The Altar, where she stands before God surrounded by family and friends.

And Him, the man to whom she is about to devote her life.

The Aisle... the Altar... and Him. Aisle. Altar. Him. And somehow from that moment on, the bride assumes this is her life's mission: *I'll Alter Him!*

Let's be honest, we all have something we'd like to change about our partner. Maybe she's too talkative. Or he's too touchy. When my wife Colleen and I first began dating, we looked at couples in restaurants and tried to guess whether or not they were married. Guys on a first date inevitably leaned across the table, tenderly held hands, and stared romantically into the girl's eyes. "See the way he *looks* at her," Colleen whispered enviously. Then she'd nod toward a middle-aged couple sitting in silence at their table, looking bored and distracted. The woman was busy on her phone, the man sat with arms crossed watching football highlights on the TV above the bar.

"I bet they're married," she said sadly. "Do you think that will ever happen to us?"

"Touchdown!" I screamed at the big screen on the wall. Colleen frowned.

I quickly pulled my eyes back to my beloved. "I'm sorry, what'd you say?"

Somewhere in the distance a rooster crowed.

I talk with a lot of twenty and thirty-somethings disillusioned by their chances of finding a partner who can fulfill their hopes for a dynamic, lifelong relationship. Many witnessed their own parents' painful break-ups and are desperate not to repeat the same mistakes. Others are miles into their marriage journey and quietly wondering, "Did I marry the wrong person?"

Whether you're single and searching for "the perfect match," or married and wondering "Is this as good as it gets?" at some point we all realize there's a gap between what we *expect* in a relationship and the reality we *experience*.

This book is about closing that gap. I've written it for four types of people:

1) SINGLE FRIENDS

Maybe you're single and feel frustrated by your quest for the "perfect" partner. Good news: I believe compatibility is wildly overrated. I hope to challenge conventional wisdom about what makes for a good match and give you fresh eyes in your search for a spouse.

2) ENGAGED COUPLES

This is the book I wish I read *before* I was married. Most engaged couples invest all their time and energy planning for their Big Day, but don't give much thought to the day *after* the wedding. I hope it will spark some dialogue with your partner—and possibly a mentor couple, pastor, or counselor—about what's involved in planning a healthy marriage, not just a splashy wedding.

3) MARRIED FOLKS

I talk to a lot of young couples who live in survival mode. Many have a couple of kids and they're doing all they can to juggle jobs, day care, school or sports. Apart from the periodic "date night," the romance has cooled, and the pressures of family life replace passion.

Once attraction fades, it doesn't take long for couples to notice cracks in their foundation. But it's not beyond repair. God's Word offers fresh hope to couples that don't see eye-to-eye on every issue.

4) THOSE CONSIDERING DIVORCE

Perhaps you're on the brink of a break-up, and you've decided to give it one last chance. You've read dozens of books about conflict and communication with titles like *7 Steps to Rekindle Romance,* but you must decide whether or not to throw in the towel.

I've been praying for you. As a follower of Jesus Christ, I believe if God can raise His Son from the dead, He also has the power to resurrect a dead marriage. I truly believe this. If you don't have enough faith for your marriage at this point, borrow mine.

If you're already divorced, I pray God will use this book to help heal your heart and fill you with renewed hope for a fresh start.

And if you're not yet married, and waiting on God for a spouse, I hope what you discover in these pages will equip you to love someone else the way God loves you.

I realize there are thousands of books about dating, marriage, and modern relationships—many of them longer than this slim volume you hold in your hand. But we designed this book to be read in a single sitting... and powerful enough to change your life.

So let's begin. And let's get real.

1

Sex and Spaghetti

Those who marry will face many troubles in this life.
1 Corinthians 7:28

I frequently sit down with couples to plan wedding ceremonies. Oftentimes, the bride and groom include a familiar Bible passage that reads, *"Love is patient, love is kind... love never fails."* (1 Corinthians 13:4-8). It's an inspiring piece of Scripture celebrating the triumph of eternal love.

But it's only half the story.

Just once, I wish someone had the guts to flip a few pages back and quote 1 Corinthians 7:28: "Those who marry will face many troubles in this life." You don't see that little nugget on a Hallmark card too often.

The truth is: marriage is hard. All spouses experience conflict, disappointment, and doubts about their partners. In fact, anyone married longer than a month has probably wondered at some point, "Did I marry the wrong person?" Maybe he's not helping around the house enough. Or she's not into sex as much as you'd like.

That was our story.

My wife Colleen and I met as freshman in college. We both grew up on the East Coast and attended school in the Midwest where everyone seemed to have stepped out of an L.L. Bean catalog—all khakis and cardigans. But Colleen grew up in Brooklyn, and I'll never forget the vision as she entered class: tan legs, neon shorts, and big blonde hair. I mean *seriously* big hair. Bon Jovi big. I'm from New Jersey, so it was love at first sight. I took one look at my Aquanet Princess and wistfully thought, "Hoooome!" We were engaged on July 19, 1997 and married exactly one year later.

Six months in, I had my first doubts.

Like a lot of men, I had pretty high expectations going into marriage, especially when it came to sex. Colleen and I didn't have sex before our wedding. We believed God wanted us to honor boundaries, but we struggled.

It was hard. So I came into marriage rip roarin' ready to go! I assumed we'd be swingin' from the chandeliers every night. Or at least every other night.

Screeeetch...reality check. At the time, Colleen was working long hours to establish a corporate career in New York City. She took the early commuter train and returned home around 7 p.m. I taught classes at a local high school and typically arrived home by 4 p.m. That gave me three precious hours all to myself. I biked with a buddy, read, worked out or met friends for coffee. It never occurred to me to make dinner; I expected *her* to do that. And after dinner, it was time for some good ol' chandelier-shakin'!

Unfortunately, most nights Colleen stumbled off the train bone-tired, collapsed on our couch, and groaned, "Can we order Chinese and go to bed early?" It was hard to take during our first few months. I felt frustrated because she was "always tired," but I didn't say anything. A friend who watched Dr. Phil suggested I express my frustration. (That's what healthy couples do, right?) So one fine Saturday morning, I sat Colleen down at the kitchen table to share my heart.

"Sweetheart," I began, "I need to get something off my chest. I have a complaint I've been keeping secret."

She put down her coffee cup and looked at me with concern.

"We don't have enough sex," I blurted out. "You're always tired."

She stared blankly and sipped her coffee before replying calmly, "Well, *my* complaint is that you're a slob. And it's not a secret. *Everyone* knows it."

I cocked my head like a dog hearing a high-pitched whistle. *Whaaaaaa?*

She lit into me. "I come home and it looks like a frat house! There's a trail of cereal on the floor, plates in the sink, newspapers flung all over." Her face reddened. "Look at your underwear in the corner! It's like living in a pig sty. Everything is trashed!"

I was dumbfounded. It took me *six months* to first suspect I married the wrong person. It took Colleen six *days*.

I walked out of the house muttering to myself, "This is the thanks I get for taking the high road? I share my heart and she attacks me in return!" My heart grew bitter. Biting my tongue, I vowed never to mention it again.

A few weeks later, it surfaced in an episode we now call "The Spaghetti Incident." That morning, I dropped Colleen at the train station for her usual daily commute. As our beat-up car pulled to the curb, she opened the door, got out and poked her head back in. "Can you do me a favor tonight?"

"Sure," I replied.

"Before I get home tonight, can you clean up the kitchen and clear off the dining room table?"

"No problem," I said.

She looked at me intently. "Tim, I'm *serious*. Don't forget, okay?"

I was offended she felt the need to question my sincerity.

"No problem," I repeated. *"Seriously."*

She gave me a quick kiss and ran to catch her train. That afternoon, I arrived home and looked at the pile of dishes in the sink from the night before.

"Ugh," I thought as the phone rang. It was my friend Jon.

"Dude, it's 70 degrees & sunny! Wanna go biking?"

I stared at the dishes in the sink. And then glanced out the window at my mountain bike in the garage. It was a no-brainer.

"Be there in fifteen minutes," I told my friend. We'd bike for a couple hours and then I'd come home and clean the kitchen. It was the best of both worlds, I reasoned.

Unfortunately, Colleen's train arrived early that day. As I pedaled up to our home, she stood awkwardly on the porch with another woman. As fate would have it, Colleen invited her friend from the train home for dinner. Apparently, she'd opened the front door, took one glance at the wild boar trail—mail stacks, dirty dishes, and pizza boxes on the table—and slammed the door shut, too embarrassed to invite her friend inside.

I wheeled up covered in mud.

"Hiya, ladies!" I smiled.

My Aquanet Princess looked ticked, so I did what any man would do. I gave my bride a peck on the cheek and pretended nothing was wrong, "Great to see ya, sweetheart!" Colleen's friend picked up on the icy reception and politely telephoned her roommate for a ride home.

Inside, I changed out of my dirty bike clothes, and Colleen went to work making dinner. From the sounds of things, I could tell she was steamed. I never heard somebody make spaghetti that loudly. *Clang! Bang! Slam!* Spoons rattled. Cabinets slammed. Colleen didn't say a word.

I sat down at the table and decided to take the high road (again). "Let's pray," I suggested innocently. "Lord, thank you for the beautiful home you've given us. That it doesn't matter if it's dirty, because it's full of love… Amen." (I can be devious.)

Colleen silently twirled spaghetti on her fork.

"What's wrong?" I asked innocently.

Eyes welling with tears, she looked up and said, "I asked for a simple favor and you completely blew me off."

"What's the big deal?" I scoffed. "There's more to life than a clean house."

She stopped twirling her noodles and waved her fork at me like a conductor's baton.

"You. Blew. Me. Off."

To add emphasis, she flicked her fork at my face after every word:

You. *Flick*. Blew. *Flick*. Me. *Flick*. Off. *Flick*.

As fate would have it, we had pasta with red sauce that night. With each flick, marinara sauce polka-dotted my face. *Flick, flick, flick.*

I wiped it off with a napkin and chuckled in annoyance, "Don't flick your fork at me, okay?"

Colleen leaned in. "It's my fork." *Flick*. "And if I wanna flick it," *Flick* "I'll flick it!" *Flick*.

And she flicked it one more time for good measure. Marinara sauce was running down my face. Something snapped. I never had my buttons pushed precisely that way. Impulsively, I thrust my hand into my own plate of pasta, grabbed a fistful and growled, "You think flicking is funny?"

Colleen's eyes narrowed. "I do."

Just six months earlier, she'd uttered those same two words at the altar.

I squeezed the spaghetti in my hand and sauce dripped down my forearm. "Would you like me to flick this at you?" I laughed maniacally.

"Go ahead," she dared. "It'll just add to the mess you *always* leave around here."

Somewhere deep inside, my man-wires crossed and

short-circuited. I wish I could say I took a deep breath and prayed for restraint. But I'm a pastor and can't lie. The truth is, the Devil entered me. So like any self-respecting man who still had a decent pitching arm from college wiffle ball, I reared back and let that handful of noodles fly toward my bride! Fortunately, the spaghetti flew over her shoulder and hit the back wall like a shotgun blast of pasta... *Sssplaaaaat!* It stuck for a brief moment and slid slowly toward the floor.

Shock covered Colleen's face. She looked at the noodles on the wall. Then back at me. Back to the spaghetti. Back to me. Then she did the unimaginable. She started laughing. Hysterically. *At me.*

I seethed. I saw red. In five minutes I'd become convinced my loving bride was my mortal enemy. I snapped. I sinned. I threw spaghetti.

That was our first fight. (For the record, I repented and have never thrown spaghetti since. Now I only toss linguini.)

THE FOO FACTOR

That night Colleen called her dad crying, "Tim doesn't take care of the house or me!"

Her dad, a quick-tempered Irishman who married an Italian, was outraged.

"Pack your bags," he barked. "You can move back home with us. We'll clear out your old bedroom and get the marriage annulled."

Colleen sobbed. Sadly, divorce runs deep on my in-law's side of the family. Some have divorced two and three times and they're not afraid to play that card in a crisis. It confirmed another truth I suspected: My in-laws were outlaws.

That was my introduction to the Foo Factor. *Foo* stands for *Family Of Origin*. We all come from different family backgrounds and have different ways of dealing with conflict…or not. We drag that baggage right into our relationships.

Colleen and I went to see a marriage counselor who told me, "Tim, picture it this way: When a couple climbs into bed, it's never just the two of you alone. Imagine there are six people in bed: you, your wife, your dad and mom, and her father and mother."

That cured my bedroom fantasies real quick.

I'd like to say things improved, but there's no magic wand for deeply ingrained patterns of behavior. Things went from bad to worse because of our family backgrounds. As an Irish/Italian mix, Colleen raised her voice and motioned wildly with her hands whenever we argued. But I was raised in a stoic home by Dutch parents who rarely showed emotion. In their forty-nine years of marriage, I can't remember voices ever being raised. In my family, the angrier you felt, the quieter you got.

When Colleen raised her voice, I withdrew into a shell and looked at her with judgment. "Who is this woman popping crazy pills?" My smug self-righteousness didn't help.

For our first five years, it was a tough go. We struggled. We fought. We hurt one another. And though we never said it, I know there were times both of us laid awake silently fearing the same thing: *"I married the wrong person."*

And you know what? In some ways, we did. As theologian Stanley Hauerwas puts it:

> The assumption is that there is someone just right for us to marry and that if we look closely enough we will find the right person. This moral assumption overlooks a crucial aspect to marriage. It fails to appreciate the fact that we always marry the wrong person.
>
> We never know whom we marry; we just think we do. Or even if we first marry the right person, just give it a while and he or she will change. The primary problem is... learning how to love and care for the stranger to whom you find yourself married. [1]

In other words, the quest for a perfect partner is impossible. Why? Because the world's view of marriage is a mirage. Growing up, we're taught to strive for this shimmering oasis in the distance—a perfect respite of relational harmony and romantic bliss. The truth is, those who marry only see the tip of the iceberg. During courtship, we tend to amplify the endearing traits of our beloved—*how sensitive she is! how patient he seems!*—and extrapolate them. Yet, as Hauerwas notes, the stresses of marriage inevitably reveal cracks and fissures we can scarcely imagine while dating. Nobody can predict how a job loss, sickness, depression, or child with special needs will impact his or her partner over time.

But there's more to making love last than surviving crises or glossing over personality quirks. According to the Bible, there's one basic problem with marriage: it always involves two sinners. "What causes fights and quarrels among you?" asks the apostle James. "It is because each of you want your own way and don't get it" (James 4:1-2). He got that right. From the Bible's perspective, sin and selfishness make us all incompatible.

THE MYSTERY OF MARRIAGE

So is there hope for couples struggling to make it work? Is there hope for singles wanting to find a soul mate, but who feel wary about picking poorly? I believe there is hope, and the Bible shows us the way. In the New Testament's most pointed teaching on the subject, the apostle Paul described marriage this way: "A man will leave his father and mother and be united to his wife, and the two will become one flesh. This is a profound *mystery*..." (Ephesians 5:31-32).

The first five years of marriage for Colleen and me were just that—a mystery! We didn't have a clue how to make love last. Many nights we went round-and-round in an argument, circled back, thought we had it worked out...and boom! We'd hit a landmine and end up back where we began. We read books on communication and concluded, "I don't understand why God wired us so differently. This is a mystery!"

But God's Word doesn't call marriage a "mystery" to rub our noses in it. Rather, the Bible spotlights a hidden truth that unmasks the folly of our culture's quest for the perfect partner. Scripture illuminates the true purpose of marriage to anyone humble enough to admit their need for divine guidance.

Colleen and I have discovered the secret. Once you admit that sin makes you *both* incompatible from the start—in essence, admit *you* are the wrong person too—it sets you free to love your spouse with all their flaws and weaknesses, and rely on God to fill the gaps between expectation and reality.

It's not magic. It takes hard work and dependence on the Holy Spirit, but God's Word offers fresh hope for making love last.

So what's the secret? We'll unpack God's truth about lasting love, but first let's examine our generation's current approach to love, sex, and the whole shebang.

Let's Chat

We designed this book to spark honest conversations among those who are single, married, or find themselves single again. At the end of each chapter, we've included a few questions to help us all get a jumpstart.

Now don't rush through these. The goal isn't to fill-in-the-blanks with the "right answer," but to be authentic, humble, and invite God's Spirit to speak to your heart. Remember to give your partner and others plenty of respect and room to share honestly.

CHAPTER 1
SEX AND SPAGHETTI

1. In the "Spaghetti Incident," do you resonate more with Pastor Tim or with Colleen? Why? How is conflict handled in your family?

2. As you think about your own Family Of Origin (FOO), what are some of the *gifts* that you bring or will bring to a marriage?

3. And what are some of the *challenges* in the baggage you bring from your FOO?

4. Stanley Hauerwas says the primary problem of marriage is "learning how to love and care for the stranger to whom you find yourself married." Think of a couple you know well who've been together for more than a decade. Can you recognize specific ways in which each partner is—quite literally—a different person than the one who walked down the aisle? Elaborate.

5. From what you know, has this couple discovered "cracks and fissures" revealed through marriage that were unrecognizable otherwise? If you're married, are there "cracks" you've discovered about *yourself* in marriage? (If you're not yet married, brace yourself!)

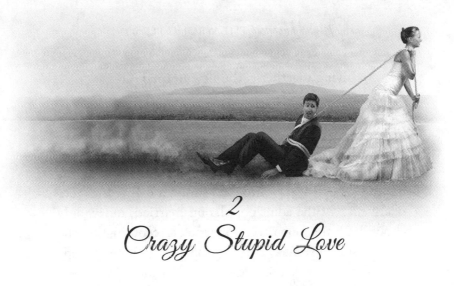

2
Crazy Stupid Love

*Marriage is a wonderful institution, but
who wants to live in an institution?*
GROUCHO MARX

OUR GENERATION GREW up in a culture of hookups, friends with benefits, and no-fault divorce. You don't have to be a social scientist to realize traditional marriage as an institution is in a freefall. By any measure, the state of our unions is tanking. Consider these four breathtaking trends:

- Fewer people get married
- Divorce is on the rise

- Living together is the new normal
- Single parenting has skyrocketed

DECLINE IN MARRIAGES

Over the last forty years, the overall number of adults getting married has dropped dramatically. In 1960, nearly 70% of the adult population married; today, only about half the population marries. According to the Pew Research Center, the drop-off is even more precipitous for the Millennial generation. In 1960, over two-thirds (68%) of all twenty-somethings married. Today, barely over a quarter (26%) marry.[1] That's a forty percent decline in the span of a single generation! And that's where we're headed: a "single generation." For the first time in our nation's history, the majority of adults (18+) will soon be single.[2] My friend Mark, who moved back in with his parents at the age of thirty, typifies this trend. He works on Wall Street, dates prolifically, and lives at home. Call it *failure to launch* or *fear of commitment*, but many adults are choosing to get married much later in life or not at all.

INCREASE IN DIVORCE

While there's an overall decline in marriage, there's an alarming increase in divorce. The divorce rate has *doubled* since 1960; nearly half of all marriages now end in Splitsville.[3] Interestingly, that statistic is relatively consistent inside and outside the church. Religious affiliation is simply not a significant predictor in whether couples stay together.

In the church where I serve, we welcome divorced folks with open arms. We don't condemn, but extend deep compassion for the hurt they've experienced, striving to be a place where families can heal. Many of my single friends witnessed their own parents' painful breakups and are wary about making the same mistakes.

As a pastor, I talk to a lot of twenty and thirty-somethings who would like to be married some day, but are pretty cynical about their chances of having a stable, fulfilling marriage. As Martin told me, "My parents got divorced when I was fifteen. Both sets of grandparents are divorced. If my chances of a lasting marriage are fifty-fifty, why bother flipping the coin?" Even optimistic Millennials fear that if a marriage lasts, it will eventually grow boring and routine.

This spirit of our age was captured in the popular movie *Crazy Stupid Love*, featuring a middle-class married couple named Cal and Emily (played by Steve Carell and Julianne Moore). Cal and Emily have been married more than two decades, but their marriage is boring and joyless. They just go through the motions as they raise their kids in the suburbs. In one restaurant scene, they sit staring at their menus with nothing to say. They struggle to make small talk.

> Cal: Oh! So full. You were right, I shouldn't
> have eaten all that bread. Wanna split a dessert?
> *[Emily is silent]*
> Cal: You okay? You seem a little off.
> Emily: Yeah, I'm just trying to think about what
> I want.
> Cal: Yeah, me too. Why don't we just say it at
> the same time? One, two, three…
> *[at the same time]*
> Emily: I want a divorce.
> Cal: Crème brulee!
> *[Cal looks up in shock]* [4]

As his marriage unravels, Cal befriends a handsome, twenty-something ladies' man named Jacob (played by a handsome, twenty-something actor named Ryan Gossling). Jacob takes Cal under his wing and begins an extreme makeover—teaching Cal how to dress like a playa and pick up women in trendy bars. The surprise occurs when Jacob reveals how sad and lonely his single life really is. Yes, he has erotic sex with exotic partners, but he longs for a stable woman to share his life. Both men secretly want to trade places with the other. *Crazy. Stupid. Love.* In some ways, the current generation views monogamous marriage like this. You can either be married and bored. Or single and lonely. Those are the only two choices many young adults see.

COHABITATION

It's no surprise then that more than half of adults live together before getting married today. Cohabitation in America increased *by more than 1,500 percent* in the past half century. In 1960, very few couples lived together. But today, the majority of young adults in their twenties will live with a romantic partner at least once, and more than half of all couples will live together before trying marriage.[5]

Because young adults often view marriage as boring or restrictive, they opt for something in between: *friends with benefits.* Living together seems to make sense. Couples reason: it's cheaper, convenient, and seems like a logical way to test for *chemistry.* They split the rent, sharing a bed and a toothbrush without the entanglements of commitment. If it doesn't work out? No harm, no foul. Everyone can just move on.

The flaw with this approach is something secular researchers describe as the phenomenon of "sliding, not deciding." In a revealing article in *The New York Times,*

Meg Jay, a clinical psychologist at the University of Virginia, described it this way:

> Moving from dating to sleeping over to sleeping over a lot to cohabitation can be a gradual slope, one not marked by rings or ceremonies or sometimes even a conversation…Women are more likely to view cohabitation as a step toward marriage, while men are more likely to see it as a way to test a relationship or postpone commitment.[6]

In other words, couples who move in are rarely on the same page about marriage from the beginning. Instead of agreeing to intentionally progress the relationship itself, they settle for "sliding into" a domestic arrangement for convenience's sake. Jay notes that the simple slide can feel exhilarating at first, "After years of living with a roommate's junky old stuff, couples happily split the rent on a nice one-bedroom apartment. They share wireless, pets, and enjoy shopping for new furniture together." However, these same benefits make the decision to part ways difficult. She cites the feelings of a young woman named Jennifer who felt her boyfriend never really committed to her:

"I felt like I was on this multiyear, never-ending audition to be his wife," she said. "We had all this furniture. We had our dogs and all the same friends. It just made it really, really difficult to break up. Then it was like we got married because we were living together once we got into our 30s."

After living together for more than four years, Jennifer and her boyfriend threw a lavish wine-country wedding. Less than a year later, she found herself looking for a divorce lawyer. In a sad twist, sliding into living together, can be more dangerous than committing to lifelong marriage.

SINGLE PARENTING

The final trend in modern culture is a rise in single parenting. According to *The Washington Times*, fifteen million American children—roughly one in three—now live without a father.[7] These kids live without a stable male influence in their home while Mom plays dual roles of nurturer and disciplinarian.

Because these children lack a model for shared responsibilities or conflict resolution, there's a lower likelihood of establishing their own healthy marriages.

This is an issue close to my heart. If you're a single parent,

I wish I could jump through these pages and hug you—you are my hero! My wife Colleen was raised by an incredible single mom, and I have her to thank for the intelligent, stable, caring person my wife is today. At our church, we have a huge heart for encouraging single parents and providing the extended family support we all need.

But if you simply look at these four trends—decline in marriages, increase of divorce, rise of cohabitation, and single parenting—you have to admit the evidence is alarming. By any scientific measure, the state of our unions is not healthy. Traditional marriage is crumbling and, whether you're married or not, one sees why our generation feels a growing disillusionment with marriage in general. But it wasn't always like this. What happened?

············ *Let's Chat* ············

Living together, divorce, and single parenting can be touchy subjects. Let's take a risk and discuss them honestly.

CHAPTER 2
CRAZY STUPID LOVE

1. Why do you think many young adults are choosing to get married later in life or not at all? Just a generational trend? Or something more?

2. Just about everybody is impacted by divorce in some way. Describe your experience.

3. How does your family's history impact your current feelings toward marriage? Does it make you fearful or confident? Does it raise any flags? What are some behaviors from your parents you'd like to repeat? What are some things you hope to avoid?

4. Some folks think living together is no biggie. Others see it as a risky proposition. What's your view? What is God's view?

5. Pastor Tim suggests God has special compassion for single parents. Have you seen evidence of this in your experience?

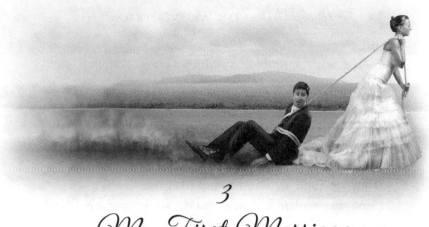

3
Mc-First Marriage

You complete me.
RENE ZELLWEGER AS DOROTHY BOYD,
TO TOM CRUISE AS JERRY MCGUIRE
JERRY MCGUIRE

ONY AND ASHLEY are dear friends and almost impossible not to love. He's from Brooklyn and she's from Kentucky. They embody the very essence of the old adage: *opposites attract.* It's the second marriage for Tony and by all accounts, they've done a wonderful job blending their families. Together they serve at our church, participate in a Bible Study, and volunteer to help underprivileged kids in our community.

But they came to see me one Wednesday, hot and

bothered with a problem. Ashley is super stylish and speaks in a southern drawl.

"Ima gonna til you how it is, Pastor Tim," she began as Tony collapsed back on the couch next to her in my office. She narrowed her eyes and glared at her husband, "Tony lies. He lies like a baaaad Persian rug."

Tony let out a sigh and rolled his eyes.

"Lemme explain," Ashley said, launching into her monologue. "Have you heard of Tory Burch?"

I shook my head no. She went on to describe how she'd been shopping at the mall and seen a pair of designer shoes she liked.

"They're wedge heels by Tory Burch," Ashley informed me. "And they're beautiful."

"They're expensive," Tony chimed in.

"They're GORE-geous," she corrected him with a laser look. "I told Tony I *wanted* those shoes. And he said if I gave him what *he* wants, then he'd give me what I want."

I looked at Tony. Tony stared at the floor. Ashley continued, "Since my husband's such a perv, I knew it was gonna be sumthin' sexual cause he's always clawin' at me anyway."

"So I made her an offer she couldn't refuse," Tony smirked.

They proceeded to outline the details of the agreement they worked out. Ashley would be sexually available to

Tony for thirty-six hours to do "whatever he wanted." In return, Tony would buy the Tory Burch shoes for Ashley.

"Basically, I agreed to be his sex slave," Ashley summarized. "Which I'm fine with. Long as I get those shoes."

I didn't quite know what to say. This isn't the kind of thing they prep you for in Pastoral Counseling 101.

Ashley continued.

"So I went along with his little sex games," she said. "For thirty-six hours the candy store was *open* and Romeo here had his fill." Then her face turned dark. "But then! Tell 'em what you said," she hissed and poked Tony in the ribs.

Tony shrugged sheepishly, "I told her I felt she didn't put her best foot forward."

"Can you believe it?" Ashley stormed. "I honored my part before God, but he didn't hold up his end of the bargain!" She was furious. It wasn't the fact that her husband promised to essentially pay her for sex. Rather, she grew livid because Tony didn't buy her the shoes.

So she called her mother in Kentucky, who cautioned her, "Just let it go. Don't get revenge or the devil'll get in there."

"Not on your life," Ashley replied. "He's gonna pay for this. The candy store is *closed* for a looooooooong time." She jabbed Tony in the chest, "I am cutting you off, mister."

Tony hung his head.

Suddenly, he looked up with a twinkle in his eye. "Ashley's upset, Pastor, no doubt," Tony began in his Brooklyn accent. "But there's a silver lining."

Apparently, Ashley's mother felt so concerned about the growing rift in her daughter's marriage that she wired Ashley $300 so she could buy the Tory Burch shoes she coveted.

"Lemme get this straight," I said, sorting the details in my head. "Your mother sent you money to buy the shoes anyway?"

"I'm wearing them now," Ashley said sticking out her foot for inspection. "Aren't they gorgeous?"

"In Brooklyn," Tony winked at me, "that's what we call a win-win."

HOW DID WE GET HERE?

Every marriage is a mystery. Most couples make compromises, little trade-offs here and there to get what they need. Or rather, what they *think* they need. For some, a relationship offers relief from the aching loneliness of singlehood. For others, it's financial security. A chance to be taken care of. Or a regular outlet for sex.

In our finer moments, we might mention the loftier ideals of family, children, and self-sacrifice. But as Tony and Ashley demonstrated, more and more couples today settle for a *quid pro quo* arrangement, where one agrees to give the other what he or she wants—as long as they get something of equal value in return.

Needless to say, this is not God's idea of mutual sacrifice. Over the last few decades, our culture has experienced a dramatic shift in the understanding of marriage's primary purpose. For thousands of years in Western civilization, we based our view of the sacrificial nature of monogamous marriage on God's Word. In Genesis, the Bible opens with the wedding of the first man (Adam) to the first woman (Eve), who God created and brought together for companionship. In God's mind, it was "not good for man to be alone" (Genesis 2:18). So God brings the couple together for two primary purposes:

1) PROTECTION

God charges Adam with the care and protection of his wife. He fashions Eve from Adam's rib so she remains close to his heart and side-by-side as an equal partner in the relationship. Two become "one flesh" and weather the storms of life together.

2) PROCREATION

God's original blessing to "be fruitful and multiply" (Genesis 1:28) is at the core of marriage. Sex is God's idea and, far from being a prude about it, God encourages it for the creation of children and our enjoyment! In God's design, family is foundational to human flourishing.

These basic purposes of marriage went unquestioned for hundreds of years in Western culture. We didn't see marriage as a legal *contract* or piece of paper to be filed with the state for tax purposes. Rather, we regarded marriage as a divine *covenant* between three people—man, woman, and God—to whom they pledged to love and serve each other "for life" out of a higher devotion to their Creator. Everyone understood marriage required *self-denial*—one would have to give up certain things to serve their spouse and kids.

SHIFT HAPPENS

But a new worldview changed all this in the seventeenth and eighteenth centuries. The Enlightenment, a cultural movement that first began in Europe and later spread to America, shifted the view of marriage dramatically. Challenging traditional understandings of faith and family, the Enlightenment put the emphasis on the *individual*. Although this resulted in many advances in learning and science, it had a devastating impact on marriage. Emphasizing self-*fulfillment* rather than self-*sacrifice*, the Enlightenment severed marriage's historic connection in service to God, the family, and the greater good of society.

Marriage, in other words, became about *me*. I should be free to choose the partner or lifestyle that most fulfills *my* personal needs. Instead of finding meaning through self-denial (i.e. giving up certain freedoms that inevitably wane with marriage and parenthood), men and women began to pursue their own emotional, material, and sexual fulfillment.

This shifted the purpose of marriage from protection and procreation to:

1) PREFERENCE

I want somebody who "completes" me.

2) PLEASURE

And you better be a freak in bed too.

Forget God's designs for marriage. Forget kids. Forget community. It's all about me: my needs, my desires, and my personal satisfaction. The Enlightenment shook marriage from its spiritual moorings and redefined its purpose as self-gratification. In other words, your spouse exists to serve *you*. Help *you* get what *you* want—whether it's Tory Burch heels or torrid sex.

In a provocative article titled "The Happy Marriage is the 'Me' Marriage," *New York Times* columnist Tara Parker-Pope observed:

> For centuries, marriage was viewed as an economic and social institution, and the emotional and intellectual needs of the spouses were secondary to the survival of the marriage itself. But in modern relationships, people are looking for a partnership, and they want partners who make their lives more interesting.[1]

Pope calls this process "self-expansion," when one looks to their partner to enlarge their world and provide a never-ending list of new experiences. Whether it's a weekend away, a new restaurant, new friends, or social mobility, the expectation is that your partner will make *your* life better.

In other words, the expectations of modern marriage are clear: you won't be happy until you find someone who is

Physically attractive

Intellectually stimulating

Romantically creative

Emotionally supportive
Financially secure

He or she should share your passions and *exceed* your dreams and aspirations. On top of it all, he or she better be "low maintenance." Heaven forbid, they have any needs of their own interfering with their primary purpose to shower you with love, respect, affection, and support.

Singles, therefore, have an impossible assignment: finding a man or woman who doesn't exist. Anyone who visits online dating sites knows if it sounds too good to be true, it probably is. Just take a moment to Google "expectation vs. reality" in the online dating universe. A study conducted by researchers at Cornell University found that eighty percent of online daters lie about their height, weight, or age.[2]

My single friend, Jim, typifies the dilemma. Jim complained to me about the lack of "quality women" in our church of over 3,000 people.

"I feel like I'm looking for a needle in a haystack," he lamented.

When I asked Jim what exactly he looks for in a woman, he described a buxom blonde over 5'10", who shares his passion for kayaking and zip lining in Costa Rica.

"Is that it?" I asked after he recited his laundry list.

Realizing how superficial his requirements sounded,

Jim quickly added, "Of course, I hope she's a woman of faith too, Pastor."

"So, basically, you're looking for a Victoria's Secret model who loves the Lord?" I asked.

He laughed nervously. Pretty much.

LIFEGUARD OR ASTRONAUT?

Not surprisingly, many single people are paralyzed about their potential pick of a partner. A recent TV commercial for Axe deodorant perfectly captures this ridiculous quest for the idealized mate. The ad features a bikini bombshell model enjoying a day at the beach. As she enjoys a swim in the ocean, a shark attacks her. Fortunately for her, a tanned, toned, and buffed lifeguard leaps down from his chair, rushes into the water, fights off the shark and heroically carries his trembling beauty back to the beach. As he lays her down on the sand, their eyes lock and romantic music swells. It is a "happily ever after" moment with two physically perfect specimens.

But suddenly, the girl's eyes dart over her savior's shoulder. Who's this coming across the parking lot? Out of nowhere, an *astronaut* appears! She brushes past the square-jawed lifeguard and runs in slow motion toward the space explorer. The commercial ends with the words, "Nothing beats an astronaut."[3] It's a tongue-in-cheek commercial that captures the postmodern anxiety many singles feel. What if I settle for someone *good*... but someone *better* comes along? Ladies, why settle for a *lifeguard* when you can have an *astronaut*?

These fantasy ideals warp our expectations in a profound way. As the National Marriage Project states:

> A pornographic media culture contributes to unrealistic expectations of what their future soul mate should look like. Influenced by sexy images of young women on MTV, the Internet, and... Victoria's Secret specials, men may be putting off marriage to their current girlfriend in the hopes that they will eventually find a combination "soulmate/babe."[4]

Indeed, magazines like *Maxim* and *Cosmo* have hijacked our generation's brains and hardwired a desire for runway models with a degree in rocket science. In the end, no one is good enough. Because we carry these idealized pictures in our head, many singles let perfectly suitable, potential mates pass by.

Similarly, it's one of the reasons married couples feel disillusioned or dissatisfied with their own relationships. The moment conflict arises, or a spouse reveals weakness or shortcomings, they look over their shoulders to see how they might upgrade. You thought you married the man of your dreams, but then discover Prince Charming has hemorrhoids and halitosis. Or your "hot babe" is prone to anxiety and panic attacks. Ten years into marriage, the lifeguard has love handles. But look, there's an *astronaut!*

Personally, I don't like the astronaut commercial. But I did see one that is far more honest about what "real marriage" looks like. A commercial for Fox Sports shows a wife setting down her groceries on the kitchen counter. Her nose scrunches up—what's that foul smell? She sniffs the grocery bag. The kitchen garbage can. And finally, checks the bottom of her shoes. Strange. Where is that smell coming from?

She walks into the living room and sees the football game blaring on the television. But no one is watching from the couch. She scans the room and her face drops. Her husband is sitting on the toilet watching TV *with the bathroom door open.*[5]

Few of us marry the astronaut or bikini bombshell. Instead, we marry the tool who watches football with the bathroom door open. Or the girl who struggles to fit into her skinny jeans. We marry someone with flaws, annoying habits and deep needs. And that is part of God's design. As Philip Yancey incisively notes:

Marriage strips away the illusions about sex pounded into us daily by the entertainment media. Few of us live with oversexed supermodels. We live instead with ordinary people, men and women who get bad breath, body odors, and unruly hair; who menstruate and experience occasional impotence; who have bad moods and embarrass us in public; who pay more attention to our children's needs than our own.

We live with people who require compassion, tolerance, understanding, and an endless supply of forgiveness. So do our partners. Such is the ironic power of sex: it lures us into a relationship that offers to teach us what we need far more— sacrificial love.[6]

You've Changed

When I began dating Colleen, I thought it was important she be athletic because I love the outdoors. Although Colleen is a city girl, she played along at first and bought a new pair of Nikes. We even got matching mountain bikes! After I broke my shoulder on our second ride, she never got on her bike again. After fifteen years and a couple of kids, neither of us look bikini-ready anymore. Everyone wants their spouse to have an exotic job, making life a grand Gatsby-esque adventure. But most take a car or train to a nine-to-five job that bores them to tears.

It's ironic because a "me-first marriage" sounds so liberating. But in reality, it's self-sabotage. We worry and obsess, "I don't want to marry the wrong person." Too late—you already did!

Every single person who decides to marry, will marry someone with major flaws, emotional baggage, annoying habits, and family history. The primary problem, Hauerwas reminds us, is "learning how to love and care for the stranger to whom you find yourself married."

A few years ago, I performed the wedding of a couple at church that seemed compatible in every way. The groom reminded me of an old school James Bond: tall, handsome and supremely confident. The bride worshiped him.

In premarital counseling, I asked, "What first attracted you?"

She promptly replied, "I love that Tom's an extrovert. He's talkative and confident, which is great because I'm shy."

Two years later, the bride emailed me in capital letters: "NEED HELP NOW."

"What's the problem?" I asked.

"He won't shut up!" Janelle replied. "He never listens and thinks he's always right."

I smiled and said, "So you're discovering the down-side of what first attracted you to him?"

"No," she insisted. "We're not compatible anymore. We took one of those personality tests. I'm still an 'I' for introvert. But he's a J... E... R... K."

They say love is blind, but marriage opens our eyes, doesn't it? It also changes us. Once married, you're never the person you were originally. I hear this all the time from couples I counsel on the brink of divorce. "She's changed. She's not the same woman I married." Well, no crap. (Sorry, I'm a pastor, lemme sound spiritual: *Holy* crap.) What in the world did you expect? The carefree girl you used to whisk away to the beach for the weekend? She has three kids, put her career on the back-burner, and feels frazzled and tired. She's prone to depression and needs meds to sleep.

"Well, that's not who I married."

Neither are you. Every married couple goes through ups and downs, highs and lows, and seasons in which you have learn "how to love and care for the stranger to whom you find yourself married," as Hauerwas puts it. People get older, change, and have different needs as they grow through life.

So listen up, men: She's not the problem. Ladies: He's not the problem. It's not just him or her. It's *both* of you. You know what makes you both incompatible? Sin.

According to the Bible, every man and woman is "the wrong person" because we're all spiritually broken and self-centered at our core.

THE BLAME GAME

My friend Andy Stanley tells of a trick he uses with married couples that come to him for counseling. Typically, one spouse begins ranting and raving, "My husband does this... My wife never does that..." and on and on it goes. So Andy takes out a pad of paper, draws a circle on it, and says, "This pie represents all the chaos in your marriage. Now, one-hundred percent of the blame is in that pie, because that's where all the chaos is." He then hands the pen to the complaining spouse and says, "I want you to draw a slice of pie that you think represents *your* responsibility for the chaos." The slice of pie the person draws is never very big. Then Andy continues: "Okay, why don't we talk just about this? Let's just talk about *your* piece. The part that is your responsibility."

Guess what? Andy's approach never works. He never gets anybody to stay on his or her piece of the pie; nobody wants to own their slice of the blame. So here's a question if you're struggling with relational static: What is your piece of the pie? Have you been honest about your role in the conflict? Or are you enjoying the blame game so much that it's blinded you to your own need for grace?

As Andy notes, "In any relationship, if you can ever get the two parties to own their piece of the pie, you can make progress. But if everybody is focused on the other person's slice of the pie, you will just have chaos."[7] This is a difficult truth to swallow! I'll never forget how my marriage changed after getting my first taste of humble pie as a husband.

············ *Let's Chat* ············

CHAPTER 3
ME-FIRST MARRIAGE

1. Tim tells a real-life story about Tony and his wife Ashley, who had some spectacular shoes. Tony called it a "win-win." But Tim suggests that a *quid pro quo* marriage isn't all it's cracked up to be. Why not?

2. Have you experienced "give-to-get" relationships outside of marriage like this, professionally or personally? Did it feel secure or insecure? Why or why not?

3. How does the kind of love Jesus practices differ from this you-give-me-something I'll-give-you-something marriage? Can you give examples of how sacrificial Jesus-love might have played out for Tony and Ashley?

4. The media has created unrealistic images of who our eventual partners might be: the Victoria Secret model who loves the Lord or the hunky heroic astronaut. Where have you seen these fantasies impair people's relationships?

5. Tim suggests that these idealized images encourage many single folks "to let perfectly suitable, potential mates pass by." Classic movie plot, right? Except the protagonist always wakes up *just in time*! In what movies does the guy or girl realize their special someone is right under their nose? Can you think of anyone in real life for whom this may be the case?

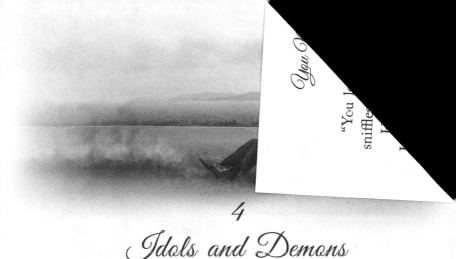

4

Idols and Demons

One of the great evils of idolatry is that if
we idolize, we must also demonize.
JONATHAN EDWARDS

*W*E WERE ONLY a few years into our marriage when I found my wife crying on the couch. Colleen is a pretty high-capacity woman and not prone to tears, but there she was one evening after work—mascara running down her cheeks, tissues balled up, blubbering to get the words out. I stood in the doorway startled.

"What's wrong?" I asked.

"You love her more than me," she stammered with a quivering chin.

I was dumbfounded. Who was she talking about?

ove *her* more than *me*," she repeated between
s.

Had she lost her mind? "I love *who* more than *you*?"
I asked. "Who are you talking about?" Was my wife
accusing me of an affair?

"That damn church," she said. "You love her more
than me."

Boom. That moment changed our marriage forever.

This happened the year after we launched Liquid
Church.[1] Colleen and I started the ministry as newlyweds
and it grew by leaps and bounds. I left my job in education
to become a pastor and found myself tending to the needs
of a young, growing congregation that now numbers in
the thousands. At the time, I worked eighteen-hour
days and loved every minute of it. Like any entrepreneur
knows, launching a business or ministry takes long hours
and hard work. It's easy to get lost in the adrenaline. And
I did.

Colleen understood at first. We had two children under
the age of five, and she stayed home with them, slugging
it out day after day, hour after hour—food, diapers, clean-
up, repeat.

Meanwhile, I had workaholic tendencies, leaving early
for the office, and arriving home late. To be honest, even
when I stayed home, I was emotionally MIA. I texted
during dinner and answered emails while in bed.

And suddenly, Colleen called me on it. My wife felt abandoned and alone. She felt I'd forsaken her and taken up with another mistress. The church.

She was right, of course. At first, I didn't want to admit it. But something about that snapshot of her crying on the couch—the palpable hurt in her eyes— seared itself forever in my mind. How did I let my heart drift and come to love ministry more than my marriage? Why did I abandon my wife?

Growing up, I'd seen dozens of leaders do this—put their work ahead of their spouses—and I vowed "That'll never be me!" But now, I couldn't deny it.

Here was the woman I promised to sacrifice and serve. The one who bore our children and was left beggin for scraps of time from my jam-packed calendar. That day, confronted by the impact of my neglect, God broke my heart with my wife's tears.

I put my laptop bag on the floor and sidled up to Colleen on the couch. We sat in silence for a long time. And then I did it. Instead of reaching for another rationalization, I reached for my slice of the pie.

"I'm so sorry I left you behind, sweetheart," I said choking on my own tears. I took her face in my hands. "I am so sorry for choosing our church over you." She rested her head on my shoulder. "Will you forgive me?" I asked.

That day, God dropped the scales from my eyes and

I started to see the mystery—and true meaning—of a Christ-centered marriage.

IT'S NOT ABOUT YOU

As we saw earlier, the apostle Paul describes marriage as a "mystery" in his letter to the Ephesians. But then he throws a curveball: "A man will leave his father and mother and be united to his wife, and the two will become one flesh. This is a profound mystery—*but I am talking about Christ and the church*" (Ephesians 5:31-32).

So you thought marriage was about *you*, did you? The secret of marriage, from God's perspective, is that it's actually not about you *or your partner* at all. Rather, marriage reflects and reveals Christ's unconditional love, forgiveness, and acceptance of us!

How much did Jesus Christ love His bride, the church? The answer is found in Christ's death on a cross. He stretched out his arms and gave his life for her! Why? Because she was *perfect*? The *ideal partner*? Hardly. The scandal of the gospel—or "good news" of God's amazing grace—is that God's love looks nothing like our fickle versions of human love. God's affection is fierce, unconditional, and comes precisely when we *least* deserve it: "But God demonstrates his own love for us in this: *While we were still sinners, Christ died for us*" (Romans 5:8).

Those five words—"while we were still sinners"—can change your life and outlook on marriage. The gospel is the startling news that God initiated a relationship with us while we were "damaged goods"—broken by sin and selfishness, falling woefully short of His holy standards. Yet, in the middle of our mess, Christ *sacrificed his life* to forgive our sin and restore our relationship to God the Father. Jesus Christ is the only man in human history to live a perfect life. And when he joined his life to ours on the cross, in a sense, Jesus "married the wrong person." He deserved better than the likes of us. But he picked you. And he chose you before the foundation of the world to enter into an eternal relationship with him. A marriage. And in spite of your sins, flaws, weaknesses and betrayals, Christ stuck it out and died for his bride. He came to this world not to be served—but to serve and sacrifice his life for ours.

According to the Bible, this is the secret: marriage reflects the gospel. And without the gospel, marriage won't work. Don't get me wrong: I believe that couples who aren't Christians have a commitment to one another. But when we pattern our lives after Jesus, he equips us to love as he loves. Husbands, wives and couples must access this supernatural source of grace, forgiveness, and acceptance if they're to have any hope of making love last. Ephesians 5:32 continues, "Husbands, love your wives, just as Christ loved the church *and gave himself up for her.*"

Sitting on the couch with my wife, the light bulb went on. The church is Jesus' bride; Colleen is mine. My purpose is to sacrifice my life to serve her, not the other way around. Taking her hand on the couch that day, I confessed my sin: Ministry was my mistress and I'd left Colleen behind. I cradled her head and pulled her close, "I'm sorry… I'm so sorry. Can you ever forgive me, sweetheart?"

The Bible calls this repentance. Repentance happens when we see our self-absorption in light of what Christ has done for us. It was a turning point for me. From that day on, I began making changes. Hard changes. Instead of leaving early and returning late at night, I began coming home early for dinner. Together, we drew boundaries around my calendar that prioritized our family first. I turned down trips, conferences, and outside speaking engagements until both our children turned ten. As difficult as it was, I learned to say "no" to the endless stream of requests from our growing congregation. (Most pastors are world-class people-pleasers and I am no exception.)

Over time, our marriage slowly changed. Not all at once, but day by day as I rebuilt trust. As I engaged emotionally with Colleen and the kids our home grew happier, our marriage more tender, and our relationship richer than ever. Instead of checking email after dinner, I left my smart phone in my bag and put on rubber gloves to help with the dishes. One night, as I tied an apron around my waist, I felt Colleen's arms wrap around me too. Then I felt her hot breath in my ear, "I think a man in rubber gloves is *sexy*."

Who would've thought?! The more I met my wife's needs in the kitchen, the more eager she was to meet mine in the bedroom! Who knew foreplay begins in the kitchen? Although my main love language is physical touch, Colleen responds to acts of service. Nowadays, when I want to get my wife in the mood, I don't bother with flowers any-more—I just vacuum Doritos out of the couch! Before we shake the chandeliers, I put out the recycling. Most impor-tantly, my internal motivation has shifted. Instead of some *quid pro quo* calculation to get what I want, I've discovered a genuine joy in serving my bride as Jesus did.

It took me five years, but I finally discovered why a "me-first" marriage never works. Sin is simply the *self*, stuffed full of self. But a real marriage isn't about self-fulfillment; it's about *self-sacrifice*. It's laying down your life for the other just as Christ laid down his life to show the depths of his love for us. And until a man or woman learns to draw on the Gospel's power—accessing the same Spirit that gave Jesus the power to love us "while we were still sinners"—he or she will struggle to put his or her partner first and make marriage last. Without receiving God's radical grace for yourself, you'll remain incapable of extending that grace to others, regardless of who you marry.

I'm convinced this is the source of the majority of relationship breakdowns: most people lack a vital relationship with Jesus Christ! Rather than loving and accepting our partner "as is," we resort to condemning, controlling, manipulating, or trying to change them. Without God to fill the deepest longings of our heart for acceptance and worth, we unwittingly turn our spouse or boyfriend or girlfriend into an idol.

IDOLS AND DEMONS

Modern culture glorifies idolatry. With God pushed aside, we look to relationships and sex to fill the void: *I need someone to fulfill me! To complete me! To always say the right thing! To be there when I'm lonely! To pick me up when I'm sad. To reassure me when I feel insecure. Can* you *do it? Can* you *do it?* Tim Keller writes in his excellent book *The Meaning of Marriage*, "It is the illusion that if we find our one true soul mate, everything wrong with us will be healed; but that makes the lover into God, and no human being can live up to that."[2]

Early in our marriage, I did this with Colleen. I

expected her to be the world's best lover, chef, and businesswoman. And homemaker and mother. Always available, upbeat, and understanding. And the list went on. In essence, I wanted her to be Jesus to me. I made her my idol. When she couldn't be the Miracle Worker, I reasoned, "Guess I married the wrong person."

And here's the rub. Jonathan Edwards observed when the object we *idolize* doesn't meet our needs, we eventually *demonize* it. So if we're single and can't find a man, we get bitter and conclude *all men are terrible*. If we're married and our spouse struggles with anxiety, we shake our head and muse, "Man, I didn't realize she's so high maintenance. Talk about the weaker sex!" Whatever we idolize—when it can't be Jesus to us—we eventually demonize it.

But if we look to Jesus Christ and apply the gospel to our marriage, we don't need our partner or spouse to be perfect or fulfill every ideal. They don't need to "play God" for us and meet every need. In fact, we have needs our spouses were never *designed* to meet! Over the last decade, because of our imperfect marriage, Colleen and I have learned to draw on God in a whole new way. Fifteen years in, sex is still important—and thank God, more frequent! But it's not everything to me. Christ offers me an intimacy and acceptance that Colleen can't give.

Colleen will tell you after fifteen years, I'm no longer a

total slob. I've learned how to hide things in the hamper. I figure if Christ died on the cross for me, I can probably pick up my underwear for her. Paul instructs both men and women, "Submit to one another *out of reverence for Christ*" (Ephesians 5:21). It's liberating to admit that Colleen has needs I can't meet. I try to listen and empathize the best I can, but I'm just a flawed man. I'm not God. That's why I'm glad she has Jesus. She may have picked the wrong man on earth, but she chose the right one in heaven.

And that's no cop-out. I don't want you to lower your expectations or just suck it up. I challenge you to *raise* the bar. Your greatest expectation of your spouse should be for them to love Jesus Christ and depend on Him *more than on you*. If your partner looks to Christ in this way, you have an excellent shot at a fulfilling marriage even when he or she has gaps in other areas. That's the God's honest truth of how you make marriage work: apply the gospel of God's love and forgive daily. Remember, marriage reflects the gospel. Without self-sacrifice… marriage won't work!

When you acknowledge you married "the wrong person"—and admit *you* are the wrong person!— it sets you free to love your imperfect partner with all your imperfect strength, relying on Christ to fill in the gaps. Self-centered love won't last. Only Christ-centered love—the radical, forgiving love called grace—can bring two sinners together and fuse them into one. As Paul Tripp notes:

When the shadow of the cross hangs over our marriage, we live and relate differently. We are no longer afraid to look at ourselves. We are no longer surprised by our sin. We no longer have to work to present ourselves as righteous. We say goodbye to finger-pointing and self-excusing. We abandon our record of wrongs. We settle issues quickly... we can live in the liberating light of humility and honesty, a needy and tender sinner living with a needy and tender sinner, no longer defensive and no longer afraid, together growing nearer to one another as we grow to be more like (Christ).[3]

What can sinner-love empower you to do? How about these everyday miracles:

- Get up with the baby even when it's *his* turn

- Clean up the dog poop because the outlaws (sorry, I mean in-laws) are coming over

- Hug her even though she went over budget (again)

- Laugh at that embarrassing story he insists on telling (again)

And that's the *small* stuff! I've also seen God perform major miracles for couples in our church including:

- Enduring the depression that came with unemployment

- Caring for a child with autism or ADHD

- Confronting the porn addiction and seeking help together

- Breaking the silence and being the first to say "I'm sorry"

Part of loving our partner "like Christ loved the church" means we step over their sin and focus on the saint they're becoming. In his book *This Momentary Marriage: A Parable of Permanence*, pastor and author John Piper offers this striking image for stepping over landmines in one's marriage:

> Picture your marriage as a grassy field. You enter it at the beginning full of hope and joy. You look out into the future, and you see beautiful flowers and trees and rolling hills. And that beauty is what you see in each other. But before long, you begin to step in cow pies. Some seasons of your marriage they may seem to be everywhere. Late at night

they are especially prevalent. These are the sins and flaws and idiosyncrasies and weaknesses and annoying habits in you and in your spouse. You try to forgive them and endure them with grace.

But they have a way of dominating the relationship. It may not even be true. But sometimes it feels like that's all there is—cow pies. Noel and I have come to believe that the combination of forbearance and forgiveness leads to the creation of a compost pile. That's where you shovel the cow pies.

You both look at each other and simply admit that there are a lot of cow pies. But you say to each other: You know, there is more to this relationship than cow pies. And we are losing sight of that because we keep focusing on these cow pies. Let's throw them all in the compost pile. When we have to, we will go there and smell it and feel bad and deal with it the best we can. And then we are going to walk away from that pile and set our eyes on the rest of our field. We will pick some favorite paths and hills that we know are not strewn with cow pies. And we will be thankful for the part of the field that is sweet.[4]

Put bluntly, the gospel is an invitation to step over a lot of crap. Not to *excuse* sin, but to face the messy business of living with a sinner and voluntarily dying to self over and over again. *Daily.* Remember, you are both chosen by God, forgiven by Christ, and empowered by the Holy Spirit. That's the miracle of marriage, Paul says, and the key to building a wrinkle-free romance.

WRINKLE-FREE RELATIONSHIPS

Wrinkle-free doesn't mean that you never address conflict, communication gaps, personality quirks, or outright sin in your marriage. Rather, the Bible gives this instruction to spouses looking to imitate Christ:

> Husbands, love your wives, just as Christ loved the church and gave himself up for her to make her holy, cleansing her by the washing with water through the word, and to present her to himself as a radiant church, *without stain or wrinkle or any other blemish, but holy and blameless* (Ephesians 5:25-27).

Whenever I perform a wedding, my favorite part is just before the bride makes her grand entrance. Everyone stands, the doors in the back swing open, and a vision in white begins her walk down the aisle. At that moment, I like to sneak a peek at the groom's face. Typically, his eyes go wide, tears well, and a silly smile swallows his face. At that moment, his beloved is radiant. Flawless. It doesn't matter if she's overweight, walks with a limp, or struggles with insecurity. She is his. And in that moment, walking down that aisle, in that white dress, she is perfect in the groom's eyes. That, my friends, is how God sees *you*. In Ephesians, Paul intentionally invokes wedding imagery to describe how God views us *in Christ*—all our sins and flaws covered by his glorious righteousness.

God calls Christian spouses to view one another this same way, not as *perfect* in their humanity, but *being perfected* in Christ. As we learn to love, accept, and care for our spouse "as is," a miracle occurs. Our radical acceptance in spite of their flaws (what the Bible calls "grace") *remakes* them. It actually has a transformational effect on their character. Listen to how this modern paraphrase from *The Message* Bible renders it:

> Husbands, go all out in your love for your wives, exactly as Christ did for the church—a love marked by giving, not getting. Christ's love makes the church whole. His words evoke her beauty. *Everything he does and says is designed to bring the best out of her, dressing her in dazzling white silk, radiant with holiness.* (Ephesians 5:25-27, MSG).

God's grace—loving us *while we're still sinners!*—cleanses, washes, and remodels us in Christ's own image. Your partner may not be Jesus, but if he or she is a Christian, the Holy Spirit lives inside him or her. The gospel teaches us to look past the surface blemishes, forgiving our partner's imperfections and stains, whether it's family baggage or sexual sin. We look past the wrinkles—the flaws and defects that fall short of our dreams for perfection.

I remember waking up one morning and looking over at my wife whose face was covered with wrinkle cream.

"Good morning, beautiful," I said as she looked into my puffy eyes.

And I *meant* it. As a couple learns to accept the blemishes of the other, they are doing gospel work. When you look past the chronic lateness, occasional temper, crooked teeth, or hairy back, and unconditionally accept the flawed humanity of another, you are doing gospel work. You imitate Christ in the most profound way. You are loving and forgiving—*and transforming!*—a broken, flawed human being, just as Christ is in the process of transforming *you* with his love. Even secular marriage experts acknowledge, when one partner begins to change himself or herself, the entire relationship inevitably changes. What's more, as a Christian, God himself loves your partner *through you.*

The Bible opens with the marriage of the first Adam and his bride in Genesis. The Bible closes with the marriage of the second Adam (Jesus) and his bride (the Church) in Revelation. That means the only "wrinkle-free" relationship we'll experience as humans waits for us in heaven. Here on earth, following Christ's example is the only way to make human marriage work if you marry a fellow sinner. (Lemme know if you find another option.)

CHAPTER 4
IDOLS AND DEMONS

1. Colleen called out Tim's surprising mistress: the church! What are some of the other idols that can tempt us away from emotional fidelity to a spouse? (Hint: they don't always have to be "bad" things.)

2. Tim says the mystery of marriage is found in the gospel: "But God demonstrates his own love for us in this: *While we were still sinners, Christ died for us*" (Romans 5:8). He suggests that five words— "while we were still sinners"—can change your life and your marriage. We see what it looks like in the gospels for Jesus to love 1st century sinners: tax-collectors, prostitutes, Pharisees. But how does sinner-love translate into modern marriage?

3. Whether you're single or married, where is one place in your life right now that requires self-sacrificing love?

4. Can you identify some of your own "stains, wrinkles, and blemishes" that a spouse needs (or *will* need!) to deal with?

5. Experts say that "when one partner begins to change *himself* or *herself*, the entire relationship inevitably changes." Where have you seen this principle at work in relationships you know? Describe.

5

Happily Incompatible

We're one, but we're not the same;
We get to carry each other.
"ONE" BY U2

COLLEEN AND I saved up and celebrated our fifteenth anniversary with a trip to Italy. In Florence, we stopped by the Duomo to see *David*, Michelangelo's famous sculpture of the young Bible hero who conquered Goliath. A towering seventeen feet of polished marble, *David* is a masterpiece of Italian sculpture—the ultimate symbol of male strength and youthful beauty. His buff physique features rippling muscles and ivory smooth skin. Perfectly proportioned, eyes pensive before battle, David looks like a Greek god in his prime.

A couple of college girls pushed their way to the front of the crowded museum.

"He's totally hot," one giggled to the other. "Like an Abercrombie model."

The other nodded in agreement and motioned to his backside, "Nice butt!"

She glanced sideways and—ignoring the No Photos sign—leaned over the rope and snapped a selfie with his sculpted buttocks. A frowning guard quickly shooed them away.

I wish they stayed to hear the real story behind *David's* origin. According to historians, Michelangelo carved his masterpiece out of an abandoned block of marble nobody else wanted. The rock was quarried forty years earlier, chipped and flawed, and considered unsuitable for a biblical sculpture. A previous artist had gouged a huge hole in the middle. Even da Vinci inspected the stone and took a pass on it. The flawed piece of marble sat abandoned in a courtyard, neglected for a quarter century.

Michelangelo was only twenty-six years old when he took the block of marble into his studio and began chipping away. Chip and polish. Chip and polish. "Every block of stone has a statue inside it," he said, "and it's the task of the sculptor to discover it." Three years later, the art world was mesmerized as he unveiled his iconic masterpiece.[1]

CARVE OUT THE ANGEL

In today's manic quest for the "perfect" partner, so many singles fixate on the externals: *How tall is she? Does he make a good income? What color is her hair? Does she kayak?* This crazy checklist causes them to overlook a whole host of suitable partners with buried potential at the core.

The Bible describes Jesus this way: "He had no beauty or majesty to attract us to him, nothing in his appearance that we should desire him" (Isaiah 53:2). So what did Jesus have? Answer: Humility. Compassion. Character. A willingness to sacrifice and serve others first. All the things that mark true greatness in God's eyes. Although Jesus was ignored and scorned for thirty-three years, "the stone that the builders rejected has become the cornerstone" (Luke 20:17; Psalm 118:22).

Now, when I coach single friends in their quest for a partner, I tell them to follow Michelangelo's example: find an overlooked piece of marble with potential for greatness, and begin chipping away. Christ-like character is the cornerstone of any lasting relationship. But you have to look beyond the surface to draw it out. When I first asked Colleen out on a date, she declined.

"I'd love to," she smiled. "But I'm busy Friday night. I'll be in prison." (I'd been turned down before, but I'd never heard that excuse!)

She went on to explain how she tutored teenage girls who were incarcerated at Illinois Youth Facility on Friday evenings.

I was intrigued. What kind of girl spends her weekends teaching imprisoned teens to read?

I'll admit I based my initial attraction largely on Colleen's big hair and tan legs. But as I got to know her soul, I saw something deeper: a Christ-like compassion for hurting people and a joy from loving and serving them. I didn't grow up with this kind of outward focus, and it was beautiful to me. Colleen's merciful heart drew me in and now—over two decades later—it has deeply shaped my own passion and inspired our entire church's ministry to marginalized people (the homeless, the addicted, single parents, and children with special needs).

When asked how he crafted such consistently divine sculptures, Michelangelo said, "I saw the angel in the marble and carved until I set him free." Part of the gospel work of marriage requires chiseling out your partner's hidden beauty, which may appear only partially visible when dating. I counsel singles to look beyond the surface and carve out the masterpiece. Does it really matter what kind of car he or she drives? Ask a better question: *What kind of father or mother will he or she make? Is he or she slow to argue? Quick to forgive? Do they have a heart to serve?* As James counsels young women, "Your beauty should not come from outward adornment, such as elaborate hairstyles and the wearing of gold jewelry or fine clothes. *Rather, it should be that of your inner self,* the unfading beauty of a gentle and quiet spirit, *which is of great worth in God's sight"* (James 3:3-4). Translation: tone down the Tory Burch and fix the focus of your relationship on the character of Christ instead.

HAPPILY INCOMPATIBLE

When asked the secret to his fifty-year marriage to his wife Ruth, Billy Graham famously said, "We are happily incompatible." I love that response. A mature man or woman growing in Christ doesn't stick his or her head in the sand when it comes to differences and relational conflict. Is your spouse perfect? Not a chance. The gospel demands brutal honesty. But it also demands radical grace that covers a multitude of sins.

"Be patient," Paul encourages, "bearing with one another in love" (Ephesians 4:2). The gospel not only refines our selection of a spouse, it also gives us grace to accept their flaws. Even *David* still has cracks in his marble. Married folks, are you disappointed you don't see eye-to-eye with your partner on certain issues? Do you harbor bitterness and a critical spirit towards his or her weaknesses? Look past the surface argument and get to the heart of the matter: your own need for God's grace. Is it possible your horizontal relationship is struggling because you haven't developed your vertical one with Jesus? Before renewing your marriage vows, you first need to renew your commitment to Christ. Only when you freshly access the love, forgiveness, and acceptance of Jesus *for yourself* will you be empowered to offer that same love to your partner. When you receive Christ's love for yourself, it sets you free to accept a spouse who leaves the toilet seat up or maxipad wrappers crumpled on the bathroom floor. The old maxim is true: you can't *give* others what you haven't first *received* yourself.

Friends, this is the hope of the gospel. Whether you're single, married, or single again, the gospel—the Good News of God's grace—is so liberating. Because you have the certain hope of experiencing the *ideal* marriage in heaven, you don't have to make an *idol* of your relationship here on earth. At the same time, God offers hope and the power to transform your relationship, starting with *yourself*. Even if you came from a broken home or experienced the trauma of divorce, God set you in his eternal family and can teach you new patterns of healthy relationships. If you ask, He can break generations of dysfunction and provide supernatural power to love in a new way.

This is my prayer for you. I hope this little book will help reframe your current relationship in light of the most important relationship you'll ever know: your personal relationship with Jesus Christ. The good news of grace makes a new model for marriage possible as we draw on God's strength and wisdom—not our culture's, but Christ's alone.

CLOSING TIME

So what's next? You just invested an hour or so reading this book and I hope you sensed God speaking to you. What will you do with what you learned? If you're married, perhaps you realized you have unrealistic expectations for your mate or bitterness in your heart. Maybe you realized you make unreasonable demands. And if you're single, perhaps you noticed ways in which you idolize a person who could never exist! Your next step is to *repent*—change your thinking and your heart. Admit your need for fresh grace and ask God for it.

Take this moment to talk to your Heavenly Father and share your heart with God. Whatever's inside, be honest and tell him what he already knows. The Bible promises, "If we confess our sins, he is faithful and just and will forgive us our sins and purify us from all unrighteousness" (1 John 1:9). This is the good news; a fresh start with God is possible. All you have to do is humbly ask.

Let me challenge you to close two things. First, close this book. Then close your eyes in prayer. Bow your head and get honest with God. Invite Christ to renew your mind and humble your heart. If you're married, I'll join you in praying that the Holy Spirit does more in your life and marriage than you can ask or imagine. And if you hope to marry one day, I'll join you in praying that God's Spirit prepares you and your future spouse to love the way Jesus loves you.

············ *Let's Chat* ············

CHAPTER 5
HAPPILY INCOMPATIBLE

1. The sculptor Michelangelo looked at a chunk of marble, a rejected stone, and saw *David*. (Actually, God looked at David—sort of young and scrawny—and saw *David*!) Beyond physical attraction, what are the characteristics of a Christ-like character that makes marriage last?

2. Where have you seen an example of a vibrant Christ-centered marriage between people who weren't "chiseled" on the outside? Family members? A friend's marriage?

3. In order to love others well horizontally, your vertical relationship with God needs to be in order.

   a) If you're a Christian, how would you describe the current state of your relationship with Christ— distant, stuck, or flourishing?

   b) If you don't have a relationship with Christ, would you like to know how to begin one? (Read *"Becoming A Christian"* *at the end of this chapter.)*

4. What's next for you? How has the Spirit nudged your heart as you've been reading this book? Can you identify one specific thing you'd like to do differently as a result? (Hint: "Be more loving" is not the right answer. Be specific!)

5. Pray. Either together as a couple, group, or privately in silence. Thank God for the gifts in your life. Confess any shortcomings the Spirit has been revealing to you. Ask God for grace to love like Jesus loved. Invite the Holy Spirit to give you supernatural strength to follow through.

Becoming a Christian

Becoming a Christian (or Christ follower) is the single most important decision you can make in life—even more important than deciding who to marry! By starting a relationship with Jesus, you can have 100% confidence that:

- God has forgiven your sins

- Your future in Heaven is secure

- You have God's Spirit inside of you forever

Starting a relationship with Jesus Christ isn't complicated, but it does require a sincere heart. The Bible makes salvation as simple as A-B-C:

A ... Admit Your Sin.

I realize sin isn't a popular word in our culture, but it's reality in this broken world. God created you and me for perfection, but we've all fallen short of God's holy standards. In other words, we're part of the problem. The Bible says:

> *If we claim to be without sin, we deceive our-selves and the truth is not in us. (1 John 1:8)*

Salvation begins by A = Admitting Your Sin.

B . . . BELIEVE IN JESUS.

On the cross, God dealt decisively with our sin once and for all. Out of his radical love for you, God the Father sent his only Son Jesus to die as a substitute for your sin. Jesus demonstrated his power over sin and death by living a sinless life and rising from the dead!

You can receive eternal life by putting your faith in Christ's death and resurrection:

> *To all who received (Jesus)— who believed in his name— he gave the right to become children of God. (John 1:12)*

Salvation is based on B = Believing in Jesus.

C . . . COMMIT TO FOLLOW CHRIST.

Becoming a Christian is not a one-time event. It's a whole heart commitment to live the rest of your life for the glory of God. Jesus was resurrected back to life and wants to live *his* life through *you*.

When you trust in Jesus, he puts his Holy Spirit inside of you. The Spirit gives you a new power to live for Christ, love others like Jesus (including our spouse!), and obey God's will.

Salvation concludes with C = Committing to Follow Christ.

If you're ready to start a relationship with Christ, you can pray this simple A-B-C prayer:

Heavenly Father, I come to you with a humble heart. I admit that I'm a sinner and need a Savior. Thank you for sending your son Jesus to live and die on the cross in my place. I believe his death and resurrection were for me. Jesus, I surrender my life to you and invite you into my heart through faith.

Forgive my sin. I turn from it now. Save me and fill me with the Holy Spirit. Thank you for eternal life and the promise of heaven. I love you, Jesus, and commit to follow you all of my days.

In Jesus' name, amen.

Congratulations, I have exciting news: You've officially joined the family of God! Through simple faith in Christ, you've passed from death to life and have the assurance of spending eternity with God in heaven.

No matter what you've done or where you've been, you can know for certain that your sins are now completely forgiven (past, present, and future) and God's Spirit lives inside you!

This is just the beginning. As a new Christian, your next step is to find a Bible-based, Christ-centered church like Liquid and join other believers in the adventure of learning God's Word and following Jesus together!

For relevant, Bible-based messages,
visit www.LiquidChurch.com
for free audio and video downloads.

Notes

CHAPTER 1: SEX AND SPAGHETTI

1. Stanley Hauerwas, "Sex and Politics: Bertrand Russell and Human Sexuality," *Christian Century*, April 19, 1978. Accessed at http://www.religion-online.org/showarticle.asp?title=1797

CHAPTER 2: CRAZY STUPID LOVE

1. Pew Research Center, *The Decline of Marriage and Rise of New Families* (November 18, 2010). Accessed at http://www.pewsocialtrends.org/2010/11/18/the-decline-of-marriage-and-rise-of-new-families/

2. Pew Research Center, *Barely Half of U.S. Adults Are Married – A Record Low* (December 14, 2011). Accessed at http://www.pewsocialtrends.org/2011/12/14/barely-half-of-u-s-adults-are-married-a-record-low/

3. The National Marriage Project, *Social Indicators of Marital Health and Well-Being* (University of Virginia, 2012). Accessed at http://stateofourunions.org/2012/social_indicators.php#divorce

4. *Crazy Stupid Love.* Dir. Glenn Ficarra, John Requa. Perf. Steve Carrell, Ryan Gosling, Julianne Moore. Warner Bros., 2011. DVD.

5. The National Marriage Project, *Social Indicators of Marital Health and Well-Being* (University of Virginia, 2012).

Accessed at http://stateofourunions.org/2012/social_indicators.php#cohabitation

6. Meg Jay, "The Downside of Cohabiting Before Marriage," *The New York Times*, April 14, 2012. Accessed at http://www.nytimes.com/2012/04/15/opinion/sunday/the-downside-of-cohabiting-before-marriage.html?pagewanted=all&_r=0

7. Luke Rosiak, "Fathers Disappear from Households Across America," *The Washington Times*, December 25, 2012. Accessed at http://www.washingtontimes.com/news/2012/dec/25/fathers-disappear-from-households-across-america/?page=all

CHAPTER 3: ME-FIRST MARRIAGE

1. Tara Parker-Pope, "The Happy Marriage Is the 'Me' Marriage," *The New York Times*, December 31, 2010. Accessed at http://www.nytimes.com/2011/01/02/weekinreview/02parkerpope.html?_r=1&

2. Catalina Toma, "The Truth About Lying in Online Dating Profiles." (Cornell University, 2007). Accessed at http://www.academia.edu/762681/The_truth_about_lying_in_online_dating_profiles

3. Axe Apollo Lifeguard TV commercial. January 28, 2013. Accessed at http://www.youtube.com/watch?v=QGoU3VH7He4

4. David Popenoe and Barbara Dafoe Whitehead, *The State of Our Unions: 2004* (National Marriage Project, Rutgers University). Accessed at http://www.stateofourunions.org/pdfs/SOOU2004.pdf

5. Fox Sports Espanol TV commercial. Accessed at http://www.youtube.com/watch?v=Apzr8f3etyU

6. Philip Yancey, "Holy Sex: How It Ravishes Our Souls," *Christianity Today*, September 30, 2003. Accessed at http://www.christianitytoday.com/ct/2003/october/3.46.html

7. Andy Stanley, *Let the Blames Begin.* (Alpharetta, GA: North Point Ministries, 2011).

CHAPTER 4: IDOLS AND DEMONS

1. Let's be honest: When most people hear the name "Liquid Church," they assume we're a cult or drinking fraternity. But we named our church Liquid for a simple reason: Jesus is called the "Living Water" (John 7:38) and we believe church should be refreshing! Dive in at www.LiquidChurch.com.

2. Timothy Keller, *The Meaning of Marriage: Facing the Complexities of Commitment with the Wisdom of God.* (New York: Dutton, 2011). I highly recommend Keller's brilliant treatment of Christian marriage to couples for in-depth study and additional insights.

3. Paul David Tripp, *What Did You Expect? Redeeming the Realities of Marriage.* (Wheaton, IL: Crossway Books, 2010).

4. John Piper, *This Momentary Marriage: A Parable of Permanence.* (Wheaton, IL: Crossway Books, 2009).

CHAPTER 5: HAPPILY INCOMPATIBLE

1. Antonio Paolucci and Aurelio Amendola, *Michelangelo's David.* (London: Royal Academy Books, 2006).